Jaimie Gusman's *Anyjar* fragments a modernist line even further, taking Stevens' anecdote to different situational certainties, fusing the lines with full-sodden sentiments that build lucidity and defy any overload of the senses. While she says, "Memory is not practical but memory is practice" we understand the serious sense of both memory and practice in these rich poems. In this powerful collection Gusman transmits a confessional pose to its sustaining direct state, with elegance and delivery: "I always hated birds... To think that I could hear you better/is to pretend that where you came from/was singular." I love the address to Anyjar—"Lover, jar, and I make three silent observances"—which I understand and affix to the centrality of these poems' themes, addressing the practicality of the lyric address and the use of fragment, quip and short lines to describe with accuracy what is utilized in the practice of exploring memory.
—Prageeta Sharma, author of *Undgergloom*

Jaimie Gusman's linguistically and conceptually deft collection, *Anyjar*, nimbly configures the sparklingly electric circuits between content and form, process and product, self and body, body and urn, embryo and mother, domesticity and domicile, witness and representation, expression and language, poetry and poem. These illuminating, intelligent, intense, and strangely lovely poems sizzle and flicker and semaphore from the dark with a magical and miraculous light held within the illusory transparency of glass.
—Lee Ann Roripaugh, author of *Dandarians*

This is a personal story, these poems. They give the reader a tangible sense of the body of the speaker. She sees with every human sense, and through her, the reader feels the back pages of another person's life and dreams. In *Anyjar* sits the conscious narrowing of experience, the conscious expansion of experience, the reorganization of that same experience. The speaker's words emerge bravely, but also vulnerably, and sometimes, they emerge with a heartbreaking quiet and hesitance. Gusman's poems are illustrations, poems that live in the art of the body and the art of the secret mind.
—Dena Rash Guzman, author of *JOSEPH*

Anyjar

by Jaimie Gusman

Black Radish Books 2017

© 2017 Jaimie Gusman

ISBN: 978-0-9979524-5-2

American poetry—21st century. 2. Poets, American—21st Century.

Black Radish Books
www.blackradishbooks.com

First printing 2017 in the United States of America

Book design and layout: Black Radish Books

Cover image by Fay Ku, 2009: "Birds Of A Feather" http://www.fayku.com/

Distributed by:
Small Press Distribution
1341 Seventh Street
Berkeley, CA 94710-1409
spd@spdbooks.org

The wilderness rose up to it,
And sprawled around, no longer wild.

—Wallace Stevens (from "Anecdote of the Jar")

All things double on one another
On to pure purpose

—Susan Howe (from Singularities)

CONTENTS

PART ONE: INCREDIBLE CONCEPTION

Lineage

The flowering waterbeds   I've dreamt of   this place
                                  abandoned boxes   the tallest
canopy of

green dust Find red and black   drums around   the oyster beds
waiting

by the shoreline   our whole lives I've dreamt

to share one   death, a life in it/s infinite   musical gesture
to swim under
                      a doom-lit death   I've dreamt
                      became heavy   as the moon
is

my iridescent wave   a good-bye

                I step over   a dirt road
                                the rippling

highway above a room   I've dreamt of beloved things I've dreamt of

my mother   the question, would I like to take off my dress   I've
dreamt of choosing two

                              stay
                              wade in the silver pools
or wave in the still   Earth,
I cannot stay   long   I say but I want to lie
I want to say

I cannot leave   cannot hang up my dress

                                        take off my shoes

hide them in mud   I want to live

        as her statue   sewn to the middle of the forest

                                   believe

                                   it is better here

tomorrow I will see you   this place

not having

                                   to remember a face

                                   any of them.

And like MAGIC Anyjar is Gone

Forgive me, he says, I took the Anyjar and buried it in snow until part of the glass froze and then I tried to break the Anyjar apart with an ax that was underneath the kitchen sink, which I discovered when rain caught the slate-stick and with one, two, twenty smashes the Anyjar wouldn't budge, which meant that an ax wouldn't do so I went to the bedroom where I found a chain-saw, revved the engine like a quake of earth and sawed the hell out of the Anyjar, but what happened next was disappointing because nothing shattered except my right knuckles and all bloody and in a bad mood I called a friend to help and the friend said *I'll do anything I can do anything to help a friend* so the friend came over with very new rubber gloves and twisted the Anyjar until the friend's hands looked like new hands but of course we thought if new hands wouldn't do, any other hands would surely fail to open the Anyjar, so then I thought extremely hard about everything and we began to make a catapult from space and flung the Anyjar into the air but it boomeranged right back only to hit the friend in the anything-but-good eye so I ran to get some frozen peas and a patch, and then I got tired so I suggested that maybe the best thing to do was to go get a blanket (take the one the dog sleeps on) and drape it over the Anyjar and just like that I sighed and the Anyjar disappeared—*so forgive me* he says sorry again, *it could be anywhere*.

Point Home

We slither by—our broken necks bambooed,
turning into art turning into trees.

Our great knees, our great mountains.
I will plant one every year you are gone and I am armed,

she says with her hips as they lighten the sand.
Her waist is barely visible, a shame (Shakespeare).

You will keep growing after my abandonment,
she tells the baby, the idea is that you won't see me.

It's eerie looking at these walls.
Hearing this water—did Keats think of this water

before his own pooled out (think of the aqueduct!),
before he could put his hand down to write it?

These walls that could keep death out.
I've put my ears to the cold sides of the Spanish steps.

Of course, this isn't the goodbye, dear,
isn't the only way to induce the sad departure.

It's not that I'm not coming back.
I will leave behind my petaline attachments.

Once skewered teeth now scatter the dirt,
end up in others' mouths.

I hear someone say, *when they go through our pockets,*
they will replace our money with stones.

They will learn that stones are worth more.
They carry more land with our bones.

The Incredible Conception

I once heard an artist compare her process to a goldfish,
the paper growing to the size of her studio.

I know I'm real because I'm not infinitely sized.
But this does not stop me from pinching other things:

the alarm clock, the snooze, the numbers,

(refer me

                                    to the morning
                    I have been alive for 236,529 hours;
                                        I need more)

the keys, the steering wheel, the accelerator,

(I pushed

                    speeding to the airport to pick you up,
                              everything requires me)

you,

                                    (as you stepped off the
plane,   as you fashioned more
                                    gait with every gain)

a suitcase

                                    (everything you
own,   now ours to closet
                                    our space, to divide)

I am not speaking to you in my dreams.
Otherwise, we are having telepathic conversations.
Two voices now row to shore:
I hear you OK?   *Okay.*
Today you looked panoramic,
statuesque.
I was saving
the white roses
placing petals
in your mouth
as anchors.

We settled—Lover and I—We slept—Lover and I—We woke.
We—negotiators of this habitat—required an other,
and so Anyjar

sat next to the pot of coffee,
on the low shelf in my office,
against the wall of the shower,
under the table in the middle of the room,
and slept by our feet.

In the morning, Anyjar reminds me
to record my dreams.

The artist is assumed to be outside of the bowl, expanding

excess.　　　surplus.　　　　overstatement.
expanse.　　　unrestraint.　　　understood.
glut.　　extra.　　　self-possession/control/discipline.
overkill.　　kill.　　　moderation.
overstatement.　　　moderate.　　　captive.
command.　　　compare.　　　order.

her palette, adjusting to the ground as it is drawn from underneath.

Explain the Anyjar

Anyjar on the sill, just jar
and I, inside and removed.

In the dream I am escaping
the narrative of invisible glass.

I try exiting, I keep knocking down
the exit, but the knocks are mute.

My fist warps its woodenness,
its woodenness warps its wood.

Not sure I am awake, my fist
apparent, like a day-kite.

Lover, jar, and I make three
silent observances. The name

of the red-head bird escapes us,
as she calls out her grievances.

Add Lover to the equation, and
is the question big enough now?

Lover stares at Anyjar these days.
I feel the affair grow into inheritance.

Watch me, as I cannot name this
inadequacy of skin or feather.

I always hated birds. I beg
the Anyjar to hold her ransom,

but ask nothing in return
as to keep her suffering quiet.

No walls to Anyjar to leave me out.
I no longer believe in the clean break.

To think that I could hear you better
is to pretend that where you came from

was singular. I explain—Anyjar is serious
yarn, also an amusing, cambering jug.

I take a swig and that moves me
so that there is room between us.

Outside are children-bandits
bicycling with bare feet.

Engines spoil the street—our walls
vibrate, but do not crush the silence.

You say that this cage is a painting.
I can hear you through the oil

petting a wing, telling the bird
to stay still, otherwise it will hurt.

Is she terrified or is that the look
of exhausted meditation?

The window does not shut,
does not open, does not sleep.

She watches; I wonder
if that's where she sees herself.

Anyjar explains—I am amusing
a design that builds as it breaks.

However the breeze pushes
the air is no direction.

Love, Anyjar

Anymore, I say, *forevermore*
to quantify and qualify so closely,
I ask my glass throbbing heart

how long do I have you?

500-1,000 years;
my life seems more nylon than ever.

> Dear bottled-brothers scattered in dirt /
> Dear cigarette butts in new concrete silk /
> Dear plastic bag, or is that your aortic arch?

> To stretch your rubber scent all over my body,
> walk the shore beside your shadowy skin.
> My captain hook piercing the ocean's big eyes

> > you sail out /
> > metabolize your half-life /
> > message me when you shimmy back /

The Anyjar's life is worth/weighs < 2 million Mountain Dews.

I slurp your sugar and swim it on my backflip   on my breaststroke

I am high on the tin-can high on the crest of your carbonate I am tuna-melt
hyped up on the dip of your fingers, Anyjar says, into my cool tunnel of quantity

> *your majesty, truly yours*

> how do I look, all puffy from love?

like a coat full of starfish /
like a ship full of sea mush /
like your fork bent to belly /

a damn thing that has abandoned the sea,
grabbing for it,
pulling it out.
No hello-ing/goodnight-ing

this is where we live,
between perpetually and extinctly.

Object Permanent

It is Tuesday. It is Sunday.
It is napkins and Windex
and garbage bags on Monday.

When I arrive the oven
is already on, burning
a place for her to stand.

She takes my hand,
puts it over her stomach,
asks me if it feels strange

and if I were to take a shovel,
could I get the illness out?
Could I help her dig it out?

I move my fingers up,
point them towards her chin.
I want her to open her mouth.

Get in my open gate heart,
get in my slow crossing heart,
let me corpse out your heart.

I tell her, whatever is in there
is blue and soaked and shivering.
Fay doesn't say she knows,

but she knows there is a flood
in the Midwestern region of her.
She knows what happens to rivers,
that the depressing days will go on
no matter how the meat is plated
or how the dishes are stacked.

Don't ever let them kiss you there,
don't ever let them turn you over,
don't ever let them shut your eyes.

I take my mother to visit Fay.
We are sweating. There are no clouds.
I tell her to say something about the memory

of being her daughter, the purpose
of these stones and that urn
is just another word for mother.

Phantom

There are some things
tight inside
delicious, rancid,
unknown to the mouth.

I must have picked
the origins, cultivated them,
smothered them, mothered
their propagations.

What sticks to tongue
makes a nest there.
Perhaps we grow
in another direction.

What if Anyjar doesn't
hold any life?
If I manage to open it
will every secret spread and change?

If I write a mother's death,
or my own sister's grief,
if I am too busy
to pick up the phone, too happy?

If I write my Lover, my love is slower.
I am two a sea.

Anyjar Elegy
for Beatrice

This is memory in exercise.
A carpool emerges a lake emerges
Anyjar and its lid.
Pitcher of Aunt Rose spills
into her hair out of her
teeth the Twist;
her favorite piano   how did I loosen if I never held

her absence?
At lunch a salad of Aunt Rose emerges
Connecticut mica and take your shoes off at the door /
her tea cold as milk.

You drive past the ambulance where your sister has died.
Only the good thing is you drive too fast to think of death.

This memory is arms above shoulders is abdomen under
spine is almost considering dust.

I visit the other graves to crave them.
How I don't need a bicycle how I don't need a bicep to open the Anyjar.

To have thought of you bodybag mass of water trouble to earth.
To scrub the routine of your lipstick off the street.

It is as I was a child singing Aunt Rose to sleep I waited singing to repeat
Aunt Rose to sleep.

Aerobics: from air; I mean, we're flying, like unpredictable magnets!
Don't you see your sister is behind you but you saw light—
half in the color of the missing half—

                              get up and get dressed
out the door with socks rolled down like foil she is crazy quick and stupid
not emerging   from Anyjar in the heat.

Memory is not practical but memory is practice.

I meant to scrub the grease down to erase.
To rub Aunt Rose down to tar.

You tell me you see your sister on the couch while we eat dinner.
You tell me you notice her as you would an armadillo in the garden.

Aunt Rose is as we are
tumble and tremble sweetly forward.

Get up, take off shoes, go to sleep with Anyjar in ear.
The conch shell gives oceans we want and wanted.

Embedded Rose. I did not see an embedded Rose lowered or othered.
I am however in recall for her piano-hair and twisted teeth.
                              I tell you
drive by again and again the kiss is an opportunity
for the engines rolling over and the pelicans watching over.
Consider your own dust as atmosphere
quick and stupid and not emerging.

PART TWO: THE HABITUAL FLEET OF IMAGINATION

Eat the Dress

Today is a fine morning
to eat your dress,

to put it on,
your shoulders narrow

like the alley where
you first learned

how to kneel
in front of your Father

while your Mother,
a house sparrow, hovered.

Origin

There is something about the *pause*
as it scratches the front door, the small door in the back, the bathroom window
standing dumb, corked, rough.

How did you get so glassy? So foggy then back to glass?

Anyjar all suited up,
from sand suitcase to smooth vase,
looks perfectly placed

(can still be held)
as perfunctory scenery: the way to make the baby/the small idea:

begin violent not to be conflict so much responsibility goes into making this or
that and if it doesn't come out right or even if it doesn't come out wrong there's
no way to tell to tell it back down to relax in your remorse to even forget when
you raised your leg opened your pelvis your fingers the palm of your right culpable
hand and to think you were wearing your only good dress pleading to make an
impression but the impression was so deep no one understood how to trace it
how to enjoy the act   (can still be composed)

The one who tried to break me
bled from his largest organ.
So there, I once said into a toilet.
So there
I like slippery wax lip-on-lip erosion.
The aesthetic of being
and being less to be something else

this crazy idea
that my genealogy is backwards

DUST	∴	MINER DISEASE
REMAINS FROM DECAY	∴	HOUSEHOLD DIRT
EARTH AS DECOY	∴	SO SCHOLARLY AS TO DIE
ARID CONTENT	∴	CONTINENT OF FAILURE

I try to figure out
here was the Anyjar
in my own voice
and it escaped

it did not change
it went from glass
to fog then back
still not human, you'd think
what is that? you'd think
the baby/the small idea
would somehow change each afterthought/is not your secret anymore

who's the captain   you think   it's me as much as it's mine

that I want it back   but then there was   the Anyjar, a professional

oxymoronic-iron-man   lift, levy, lower   (can still be compost)

you'd think it was getting easier
to give you a difference then take it away.

On Genealogy

On his knees he was begging
Anyjar who lectured us on the art of collecting.
You can tell by the curved lip this jar is a bastard
getting in our business
slamming doors
there is no father (worth a know)
keeping them shut.

(Someone must have left Anyjar
in the snow, on a doorstep,
or wrapped in newspaper afloat a river.
Someone must have stolen the keys
to an attic, where they stored the bones of a mother.)

Remind me why we need fathers,
why we feel the need to replace them
or change and not erase them?

You and I have been romantic since we met,
discuss musical instruments as we chew pen caps.
We shout at each other, a road between us
a punctuation for travel as long as ancestors' breath.

This new vocabulary is how you walked me home
that summer, to the house with the flood.
How the walking has sored us, has given us nicknames
to live by, to live up to   *sweetie pie*   *the apple of my existence*   *the executor of will*

                    bitch-wife   *bacon-maker, baby fryer*   *tit-licker*

                    shirt-stainer   *shit strainer*   *love of my life*

And now we only speak in actions,
because *if you feel what is inside that thing*
you do not call it by the name by which it is known.
Everybody knows that by the way they do when they are in love.

Things are occurrences:

open to bake   *work hard*   *pull the,*

kill/ejaculate   *remove burning*   *wash with all of her*

covet to clean   *evidence*   *is ready, open for eating*

On his knees he was begging.
I was there with his kneecaps.
Pathetic lovers, Anyjar contends
there is nothing between these two but a three,
a conviction built by that undoing.

Line up against the wall.   *Are we being measured?*
Two convicts guilty as ever.   *Command that we close our eyes.*
We shut up, reach for each other.   *Bang!   Bang.   Bang.*

I feel his hand jump. Mine still.
We don't blow that easily, our bodies bound,
mind-fucked by the position of a few words.

My own father would be running for the door.

Factoid (1):

you were being an android
avoided by light
devoid of dull statements
in a voyeuristic moment
I shook my neck in yours
so you were bobble headed
perhaps speaking a tad shakily
a shark may have up to 3000 teeth
washed up on one shore
is my baby tooth
the picture of my mother
the rope
an electric grand piano
wet but still working
you are not wet but still working
there are up to 3000 versions of light
in a light bulb

Factoid (2):

shallow water blackout
can occur in a waterbed
on a rocky surface
i.e. a coral reef
i.e. the moon ponds of the moon
or imagine your sister
went diving with her father
and almost drowned
had an anxiety attack
imagine the fish were hysterical
as she moonwalked
the ocean floor
not with a dance instructor
or your father
with a man no one knew
when the story was replayed
your father was on the deck
absently thinking
about fishing
about how many hooks
were left in the tackle box
there are as many as 3000 lines
in any given ocean plot

A Closer Look and a Long Shot

I am swimming above you.
Water-wing, space-mask, flotation-girdle:
properly suited for message delivery.

A malfunction occurs in the darkness.

I am flying tandem,
twenty pounds of letters behind me,
some folded into octopi or made into stellar spit-balls.

Some written by your magistrates and some by your majesty.
Some by partners in crime and some by the criminals.
Some from the inside and some from the outside.

My trigger cronies, A–Z and their combinations

fall out. I get lighter. Meteor showers. Things you don't want to read. Fall out. On
your face. A malfunction occurs. Darkness comes down like a spoon. Scoops of
earth. Lonely faces look up. Heavy mouths open. The king chews. Before the others
get to look. He is the magician.

Syllabic bends curse the wind.
I can see the king's children below
lined up like pineapple rows.

Boys and girls march ready:
jetpacks with fuel and silly string
strapped to their child spines.

Watch them change the world,
building up like balloons, then whack!
All weasels now; they weren't meant to be stars.

Watch them fall down, little punctuators,
hopeful thinkers with pressure blowers and water guns.
They tried. We made them try it.

We tried to rewrite it

with air space and attic access, with backfill
and baskets of caulking, with chip boards
and ductwork. Beams of light and instruments

to measure their illumination,
to give children the indication
that success equals freedom.

All disasters happen overnight.

Wake up and evacuate to the sky.

Omit the Anyjar

This must be Idaho.
The roads widen like fields.
Clouds settle into various museums, homes
surrounded by water.
The places we open do not answer.

                                          We don't have a plan to get back to our

                                                                    quiet city

                                                              continue east

                                                              to Montana.

At the dam we ask it. We make two wishes,
then turn our backs.

                                                        Levels of water rise,

I see in your eyes levels of   Anyjar
flood

changing the geometry of the landscape.

At Pizza Hut, we are not yet lovers.
The waitress is so kind not to look!

By the time we hit Kalispell the Hampton Inn looks like a home.
I stop thinking about bedrooms.
I sniff the old particles of a punched pillowcase.
Then I go dark with an old dream.

We sleep, Anyjar between our static bodies, and the next day

it is a napkin on my lap as we drive through the western side of Glacier National Park.
A frozen lake,
a pillar of ice-cubes   I swear I can drink with my bare feet

                              watch a bareness
                              belonging to my brain
                              pulley the snow

but I feel unattached
I cannot say *hold on*,
or anything.

Not-yet-Lover laughs
as I capture deer after deer with my camera,
document her muscles as angles towards his.

Not-yet-Lover insists we drive around winter towards the eastern entrance.

                                                    Like weather, he is bitter, cracks.

I exile Anyjar to the back seat of the car, as we drive toward a dead end—piles of
broken ice-people scatter along the ground—

Not-yet-Lover stops short,
Anyjar rolls under

                                                              makes me crawl
                                                              bust an elbow,
                                                              so we continue

steering wheel wobbling, the blood around my bone, the Anyjar I stuff in the trunk

echoes on the way to Missoula.

[Anyjar record this moment] [   ] [this imagination come
out like it was imagined random input output categorize Anyjar] [scramble words
there is nothing innocent about vocabulary] [   ]
["is this on yes blue lens night lens"]

(a quieter city alight)

I can see it, you said.
I see it with all my might.

Explode, Expunge, but Hold on Tight

We wake tangled in wet dream.
I am wearing that sweater and you are undone,
sewing your skin to my thread.

Anyjar a spill, ship a swell.
All I can feel is our rocking
is in sync, like a hagfish's five hearts.

The problem with our drowning is panic
reaches the surface too quickly.
We wade, then scatter from each other

tearing your skin, leaving me bare-chested
but speckled with goose bumps and needlework.
Of all the hurdles, the hardest is to gather our things.

(Our eyes met over the ocean but who could tell water from glass?)
(Our arms became baskets to carry sheets of paper, our photographs.)
(Our ears resisted waterlog; we maintained parallel swimming paths.)

There is disagreement in my thinking
that we can reach for the same possessions
and simultaneously let go.

What makes us different from our extensions
is that they are supposed to remain outside of the jar.
But we both grab at the emptiness, never enough for two,

as though we would go our separate ways
as some do after a flood or a drought or a miracle ends.
But I accuse him of planning the escape.

Anyjar, have you lost interest in our home? we ask
as our throats struggle for air, struggle for a language
we can agree upon using in moments of distress.

Silence has been putting us to sleep for years.
The roof tiles became lifeboats long ago, but I didn't expect you
to float one over and cradle the Anyjar under your arm.

Sonnet for the Search Party

Lemon skinned moon
purrs away, *only skin* she says.
In a thousand mirrored pores
sits a handful of feral stars.
Only face, why save it? Lover agrees,
hangs yellow, bangs louder
on the hollow door,
hangs his entirety: eyes, a pinhole mouth
two heart-shaped lungs
listen for her backwalk.
The first time she landed
on him, the purring rattled an eyelash
and sunk the earth like a spoon.
An echo, she says, goes on saying.

The Grandfather Paradox

When Anyjar gets mad
the earth gets low on herself,
stuffs her dress in her mouth.
Nervous habits are acquired
from years of erosion.

All other affects require
the tongue rolling over lace
covered roses, a classic embroidery.
I wore the same as I prepared
for my own eruption in formal disguise.

With a pewter fork
she slits each bud bloody.
Bouquet on the counter,
apron soaked with delicious flowers,
water holds stem to stem.

The earth feeds under our feet
while we eat our meals, I think
we must find them, the Creators.
If all we are to do is wander,
Lover chews, wonders how.

I try not to break the dishes
or tear the rug to rind.
Madness is transferrable by air,
any space is exposure.
He coughs in the corners,

folds his lungs in leniency.
He thinks I'm making a joke
by making a joke out of choking.
Some days pain breathes easily
while the house is still for hours.

I am unable to count or measure time.
We fog the windows, write
our names only to cross them out.
Our gloves cover up our temporality.
But for the Anyjar life is best

without wingspan, without wind.
In a secret telepathic conversation
Lover and I decide in a moment
that we must know where we came from.
The Anyjar cries (tears!), sucks at the air.

We drew up the plans with pencils
and protractors and thought of translating
these two dimensional images as an easy task.
But there was a period of revision, of taking
away and re-placing, of argument and agreement.

This was difficult to do with two, distracting
to do with three, although all our books spoke
for the necessity of a synthesis, of a third voice
to point us out of process and into composition.
The way a god injects himself into man to make other men.

And so the thing was built, a two-seater
with a cup holder (extra-large, per Anyjar's request).
It was made of recyclables, of others' trash
and some of our own replaceables.
The rings those things left behind were ours.

By the time we finished, the sky was not ready
so we decided to nap inside the thing.
And for a while we felt like a family,
three carp in a neatly threaded net—
how many others could we count to sleep?

We were trying to find the first woman,
the first man, and the first idea
to come between them, to find that idea
and wish upon it a mysterious death.
Push it in the thing and take it with us.

But where will I find you?
The two lovers ask one another,
when we wake up
what will become of us?
The earth comes quickly at any hour.
Anyjar has the patience of a saint.

The statue was here before.
It was cemented in sand,
made from its own memory.
It may belong to us all.
The mountains, the sea,
our single squinted face,
grief.
Today you looked limp,
letting the anchors fall
to your feet, turning ocean
floor to garden
Can you see me?   *I am always cultivating.*
Picking roses
for our funerals,   so we begin to grow back in.

Do you remember the hotels   in and out of them   old luggage
scrapping walls with our thumbnails
leaving a pillow in the shower, no money for a tip.
Anyjar is filled with change,
we are mobile as well.
The constant *do something,*
the jar demands so much already.

Picking up after this thing on the couch
makes me aware of my composition

(the one who sleeps the soundest
but monitors my sleep).

Lover manages to let blame manifest in a backpack,
to become a river
swollen with sentimental offerings:
a braided rope, a picture of our mothers,
a musical instrument—
these things only half-work.

The Anyjar is not the other half.
The Anyjar is not even a part of.
The Anyjar is not an invisible point.
The Anyjar is not a remarkable dot.

The Anyjar breastfed the hell out of me.
The Anyjar sat me down after to talk.
The Anyjar said nothing and everything I wanted.
The Anyjar could not read my emotions.

The Anyjar is not anything, not all at all.
The Anyjar is not a beginning or an end.
The Anyjar is not a negative or positive of that.
The Anyjar is now open for discussion.

It is morning in Missoula
when we hear a missile blew up the people.
We hear the news in a hotel lobby
while other people drink coffee and make waffles,
the batter dripping down in sheets.

I run to the bathroom.
I need a mirror.

Are we not essentially made of paper?
Paper thin hearts and stomachs and lungs?
Even ripping apart seems easy
as turning our backs
or forgetting to face them.

I go upstairs to take a shower.
The tub fills with water, doesn't drain.
I bend down to see the blockage—red string
in the mirror and my head is a package of yarn.

It looks as though the sun shone in the same spot
on the same muted mauve curtain by the doorway.
It is scientifically impossible for this pink blotch
of fabric to transverse the already pink blotch of space.
Get in, you say while closing the shades.
Instead, I walk downstairs

to fill the ice bucket—
leave Lover alone with the jar.
I come back to his pants rolled down,
Anyjar in his left hand
swinging and yanking and violating
(our?) borrowed space.

It was hard for me to swallow
my instinct to behave, swallow
in my stomach a pit so large
I began to eat my own dress,
a habit of environment.
I learned this from my mother.

We only become seamen because our fins corrode
when color drops from our bodies
we are all glass you say it's a big responsibility
to open up, to remain transparent, to stay solid under water.

In a painting is how I frame you how I approach a subject
without treating it like a subject affected by movement
like a demand, the viewer
has no motion to her does not get emotional.
We are not hurtful, our kind, we are various parts of speech

with impairments, partialities, inefficiencies, footages
which undoubtedly came from impairments, partialities, inefficiencies, footages.

After Note

You are panting

                                  you paint

a parade at my feet,

                                  you brush my hair

with your fingertips,
leave no strand unattended,

no part of my body   cold, not even
temperate, bound by rope   *such things affray.*

I am on deck,

                                  (you are all hands)

you call me your delicious halibut cheek.
Your knife hangs over me, you say:
sweet mistletoe.

I describe myself as a cup of water
            and you drink   sand.

PART THREE: FUNERAL POEMS

Disaster [general]

The emails have been sent / we need more.
We always need more.

I hear they are flying them out with supplies.
I hear they are already prepared.

I grab my bandages, hold them tight against my chest.
I run up a mountain / am still running.

I donate my heart to the nearest emergency cooler.
I can feel my heart missing its cadaver.

The wind is an ice-box door.
The next door will open any minute.

My heart is waiting to be retrieved.
The water returns smelly fish bones.

There is the statue of the first mother
rocking her stony baby, the marble head

sinks into her sandstone armpit.
The salt remains on her feet.

She asks for forgiveness / she is always apologizing.
Stop. Here is my bloody rag of heart.

Here is a stick and propeller.
Get out of here before I change my mind.

At the top of the mountain I reach into my chest.
I pull out the system. I push a button / am still pushing.

I put on the glove set sent from my mother. These gifts always feel dirty like a stolen disguise. Find my hands something like a frozen pudding pop it's winter unaware of time but bound by it: I am a sucker for the swirl of any claims to be distinct. I push the pudding pop through its wrapper and although this method keeps the hands warm and alive the sides of the pudding pop tend to stick to the sides of the wrapper, therefore losing precious pudding. So I approach the pop with scissors, cutting the paper tip to reveal the cold delight beneath. I lick winter's rib—no—a set of ribs, like my own spine is missing an integral part of movement. I have never asked you to lick *my* spine, but perhaps I should to get this going. I should melt into your skin, and move with you. *Where shall we go today?* these gloves gesture. It is a cruel joke to be paralyzed in the mind. But a gift is a gift I suppose, even if I take from a strange hand. Perhaps it was placed there intentionally, as if to say *I want to be here, I want you to want this*. In this way the gloves are really the perfect gift, the absolute disguise for a daughter. It is partly why winter is sexless why the snow covers everything but can't commit. Like my mother asks for "her" gloves back, nods at them. Like his aching thighs around my knuckles forcing the thaw. Like I took the pudding pop right out of my mouth to reveal that the only magic holding us all together was a stick and the memory of feeling safely tucked between air and a plastic tomb.

Descent

Father had you me in mind
when you met the earth for the first time?

Mother you had me   had you minded me
the earth was first when I was in you.

You crossed the sea
but not the wind   nor the ship.

The Dominion of the Jar

Anyjar must think: what is the very essence inside me?

Teachers say if you have no essence, then you are not alive.
And the thought of this makes the Anyjar roll around
in a chaotic tumble.

Anyjar sits, thinks
and years go by—buying sheets to cover the art, to bury it—

for no *aha* to ever come.

The Anyjar emerges from gardens and beaches, ships and cities,
with people and trees and fish and birds, and yet remains
inside a state of nonexistence.
Who am I?
The Anyjar struggles with this: tar, fog, glass.
And no matter how Anyjar dresses or undresses,
the truth remains unbearable,
an unspeakable notation to a larger test.

This confused disturbance or term
turmoil is a shiny, attractive mayhem.
The Anyjar enjoys stroking each uproar
with words, build and build
a glorifying epitome:

        aesthetically 'me'   some version of 'yours truly'

that can swim and smoke and smother itself in conceptual rearrangements.

But no, that's not *me*, cries Anyjar.
The term has ended.
No kingly or queenly awards
to so sovereignly take a high shelf.

Anyjar sinks, sulks
takes out loans.

And then, the Anjyar (finally) broke & open sings heart-filled hallelujahs.
Not being a religious jar, the Anyjar knows it cannot/could not warp nor magnetize,
control nor contract — and sings for *that* truth.

Anyjar's reign is over.
And the worst part: Anyjar's unmatchable intelligence
cannot accept the simplicity of that.
Essence is just a word and cannot tame
what I saw through you.

On How to Perform Chiromancy

To modernize the Anyjar you mustn't make it new you must make a stunning replica of a replica then destroy that replica of a replica using an uncommon weapon such as the hammerhead shark or the frayed bathrobe tie that keeps one's breasts to one's chest you must not use glue to repair the Anyjar because the world is not beyond repair but is not ready to be stuck or unstuck for that matter it is not about manners the way you lift the Anyjar to the light which might be interpreted as invasive or to hide the Anyjar under your dress (not invasive) but it is about respecting the angles because you see from a distance the Anyjar might be tall and thin and as you move closer as you want to take the beaker into your hands put one palm on one side and the other palm on the other side you will find that the Anyjar will remove your skin completely when you shake it you will scream for it to tell you where it is hiding your skin the Anyjar will notice what you cannot but is trying really trying to make you a new thing for the sake of breaking what is already broken the Anyjar will open you will breathe you will be distracted by the internal nothing and suddenly the Anyjar will shut and as you look down you will see your hands are now stuck inside yet you are holding one palm on one side and one palm on another.

Back to the Table Trick

Our friend the magician is in town.
He asks about the Anyjar, about our travels.

(How long, and how far:
depth, height, weight.)

He wants to know how we have used or misused
the object, and if we have given it a name.

(If memory also expands then might there be another way out?
If I record these destinations, if I give them nouns as if to place them.)

He mentions the delicious dinner as I clear the plates.
The magician wants dessert, complains of infinite hunger.

(I cannot tell time, measurements
are also lost.)

The magician removes the cloth under our glasses
quickly as a forest as not to disrupt what happens above it.

Back at the artist studio I watch her fuss with the sheet,
now the size of the entire room, which has been hanging mysteriously for months.

No one even tries to sneak in to ruin the picture.
For all we know, the artist has been holding the other visiting artists hostage.

I can make sense of this: the artist is plump, plumper than before.
It isn't only her belly distended, full of landscape, but her shoulders, her legs,

her ankles can no longer be seen. She gets around the room in a mobile tank.
She has a gondolier who paddles her around. She complains of an empty appetite.

I imagine she might be consuming the others, and although she has not licked
her lips in my direction, I feel somewhat plated, somehow part of the exhibition.

These precious collections impress our guests, she points to the painting.

I might like to lay it all out

unfold the goods as they get good laid out on the table get fucked like that open air.

Can you smell the sea?

Imagine how you were placed on this ship everyone comes from one

an asterisk a grammatical pause

two

a question a tricky interrogation

three

a pejorative a negative response

four

a conjunction a human quality.

As though looking out the window with your eyes pressed against the pane removed the window.

As though this were a cruise ship and I wouldn't say *window*
I would say *porthole*

As though this were a religious voyage and I wouldn't say *porthole*
I would say *fenestella*

I might like to lay it all out in order

with the largest parts at the center of the table as this is how to get properly fucked on a table.

The torso taking up most of the center, legs hanging off in the breeze.

As though sawing the material with your hands and getting splinters will have removed the material.

Is this not a mode of transportation?

Imagine you did not take a ship, but instead took a plane.

As though the speed of the vehicle sped up the world while you kicked back, put your feet on the folding table.

I might like to lay it all out make good with every thing fucked then fuck it up even more

as though committing one extremely perverted act will remove all the other moderately perverted acts.

This does not make me any more or less perverted.
This does not answer the question as to how we have used or misused the object.

At the unveiling she makes sure to hide her tools: the paintbrush,
the palette of city colors and glosses, her hands clenched as to erase

her dirty fingertips, the nails half bitten off now in her stomach.
The gondolier helps her navigate the studio as she is uncompassed,

unscaled in this space she has been swimming most of her life.
It is time to remove the sheet (the one a dog sleeps on), the people

huddle together in the middle of the room like trash in the sea.
They attach their own mythologies, roll up their sleeves.

I know this is real because the sheet comes down.
Because it reveals another sheet:

the museum in Idaho, the doll-sized

                                        (process is not epiphany:
                                        on the way to pick you up
                                        I was large and small)

footsteps, leading to the dam

                                        (nervously wet
                                        I walked in your direction
                                        uncomfortably)

we drank glacier run-off

                                        (as I could not run
                                        as I was born swimming
                                        without direction)

the twist, the twisted ends

                                        (unfolding our story
                                        then folding it
                                        then storing the folds)

leaving out the middle:

RUMOR	∴	ACCOUNT OF FACTS
IDLE SEPARATION	∴	SOMETHING SAID QUIETLY
SOUND IN CHEST	∴	CHEW WITH DIFFICULTY
EDDYING MOTION	∴	STREAM OF MILK

as if

to put the image on another surface   (transference)
to change ownership of something   (a system based on labor)
to pass from one person to another   (the state of being dominated)

a break-in   airflow   alter(c)ation   of the text

as if

the ordinary the unexceptional was the exception as we all travel stack our landscapes on our backs pull at them the idea of mobility that your memory is small and large until it becomes a unit you no longer recall or push out what's inside of it you forgot to turn it on forgot to make due with what you had as they say the baby will grow in the strangest places.

[Anyjar hit off]   [imagine the rest like you were never really there]   [inside]
[out of it or]   [   ] [when you wake up]   [when you are ready we
will be here] [waiting for you to say "   "]   ["is
really what I meant."]

Anyjar on Repeat

We play back our repetitions in the bedroom.
Hand goes there on a scrunched up face.
Other hand goes here in the bucket seat of the hip.

At this point in the book our house is roof-deep in water (ruins the book)   the jar
cannot contain it   we have searched for its family for ours   our
regions are deep   but is not religion   the paper fray   mold from the water   has
spread   You ejaculate   I exterminate (or attempt to)   We come
back   *let's try this again*   On our mattress   is an album, some pictures,
some words,   some pasts which we think   we gain   by watching our
tongues   roll around a simple bedsheet   the prop   a good show   how
many times our neighbors watched   we let them

The water has dried up—   a miracle / we own no such thing—
we've been gone for months, but time is arranged also
by memory, by what we might mistake for memorization ("the most uncreative act") /

But the memory fizzed,
creating the fuzzy grey lines
on an old tape.

Do you want to fool around?
He hits the TV,
I think we need an upgrade.

I think I understand the Anyjar
is not only a decorative or an alembic
but a systemic approach to the epistemological discovery of collective remembrance.

For instance, I was born underwater.
My muscles recall
how to catch a starfish,
how to live below a ship and still breathe.

Messaging

I open the episode to find myself in it.
(*We all do this* the others assure me.)
At some point, I rummage through a garbage pail
then another. The things I find
never seem to be what I'm looking for.

In this scene I open the basement door, unlocked
but mindful of secrecy. A heavy ocean hides there
with the potatoes, the shovels, the laundry.
I know that this is where we all go for winter.
This is where the others have stored their clothes.

(Confused as to why I am naked:
as in fully clothed but not in my favorite dress
which appears to be hanging up, freshly ironed,
smelling of ammonia and corn husk.) I am aware
that I am also not "put in" any type of skin.

A woman walks in, asks me how long it's been
since I've had a good cup of rosemary-peach tea.
My answer is exact: three years to this moment.
It is cold in the basement, yet she doesn't offer
a drink. She writes something down, walks away.

Certainly, this should be an embarrassing moment.
There are mirrors to tell me so, one stitched to my gut.
I have breasts that fit neatly into my hands,
arms in a fashionable cross-bone, a Third Reich style,
also worn by my high school sweetheart.

But he doesn't visit me here, only women are allowed.
(*Don't worry* they tell me I am not alone!)
There is one in particular who follows me
from one end of the basement to the other,
but refuses to cross water.

I fast-forward. The act is an unexpected emotional experience.
I am digging through the floorboards, but instead of wooden planks,

they are books. Underneath I find cloaks and hats.
I try them all on in an obsessive manner.
I break the mirror under my breasts.

Woman after woman comes down the stairs.
They ask me extraordinary questions about simple things.
They say *do you remember skinning your knees on the front porch?*
Can you recall how many stitches are lost in your sister's forehead?
My desire to speak lessens with every entrance, with every insistence

that there is an answer perhaps tucked in the pockets
of some ghost's whimpering lungs, some leopard print
flap cap that spreads its wings across the bricks,
breathing heavy as it expands beyond its extant form.

My grandmother steps in, asks me if I would like to play
Twister, or some other game where your limbs disappear.
We never played like this together while she was alive.
I press *pause*, and she has me pinned down on the floor.
Her hands are on blue dots, which she paints over my arms.

She asks me if I think she is pretty, if her hair is alright.
She is beautiful in a way that is undisputable,
in a way that no longer exists.
I am however a damp and swamp-like sponge
with no features of my own: I am the basement door.

In the morning I discover I am without a staircase.
The impossibility of descent, of how I came here.
The impossibility of ascent, of how I might depart.
We are only what we bring. We never belonged,
only longed to be on a windowsill, full of everything.

Anyjar on Physicality and Pain

Even apart from all things
that go on in the glassless world,
the Anyjar is emotional.

It is empathy that gets to the jar.
A terrible attack lunges toward
the Anyjar's awkward attachments.

The Anyjar imagines some hand wrapped
around its bottleneck — an image of throb
and thwack,

the violence of not knowing how the end
will take itself to the most serious corner
of the earth and go without uttering an ache.

> *This seems painful*, says the Anyjar.
> *This seems unlike any movie I've seen*, says the Anyjar.

And the Anyjar, all theatrical but sincere
cringes in the pain that is not pain.

I cannot conjure a response
because what seems is nonetheless unstitched.

So I say, *there is no symbol for the universe to unequivocally agree:*
yes, this is grief.
Put it on. Take a hefty walk.
Never stop.

How do you project this idea of mourning onto glass
when there is the insistence to *feel* it into blue,
cold, lifeless excitement? As though it were water

with its emptiness, its thrashing.
It hardly makes any sense.

The Anyjar huffs, wants the polaroid version
of things like loss, fear, and hurt—even more
than it wants happiness, success, or freedom.

There is cruelty, and then there is the condition
of desiring the experience of a deliberate pain.
And there is no general relief to gain from this insight.

Like the Anyjar, the disasters
we place on the tare are weightless.

The immeasurable, only attached to the physical,
can stimulate the solid, repetitive internal structure,
and make it shallow as a nail.

"Endings are Not a Luxury"

Lover, are we now relaxed

coffee table ready closet cleaner motivated vibrators slick on our chests are we heavy
luggage lifters quickly letting go of all this we once stuffed deep in ask, Lover are
you ready to jump out of 32 windows of pain and if so what will jump out?

Lover, are we now a synchronous reflex

rubber capped maxed out in dead bird position in snow angel location without
snow, light to outline our whitish bodies if we are lifeless we aren't kicking we aren't
schlepping groceries up three intersecting stories.

Lover and I, backs reclined, look at the world from where we are!
The sky is beneath us and we are truly breathing through this water.
I believe I can save children through the introduction of metaphor.
Father of Knowledge, our spines are better suited as bookends.

In the afternoon I am in your lap of glass cinder.
You are upright and I am sideways and sacred forever.

Imagine the ocean we collect in our heels.
We are marine-makers from the comfort of this couch,

store our darkness inside smooth mason capsules
so that the mosquitoes don't get in, so that the birds don't get in

I stack the dead against the living and scale up.
I lug pounds of petals in plastic bags

so that I may keep their contents visible to my heart,
so that I place my contents next to your heart.

I thought I heard you say *nor the ship, nor the sea.*
I thought I saw the roses were wild,

but when I came closer the angle
showed no idea I could contain.

Murmur

My heart is growing into itself.
It laps up the blood that tries to choke it.
When we were young, my sister's ears,
doctors said, were something to grow into.

My heart is like a chewing machine.
The Anyjar doesn't like the word *machine*,
says there is nothing good about a doctor
who measures the gaps in blood's beatings.

This waiting is driving me insane
my sister says after I tell her there
is no operation, no cure for the thick muscle.
You see? The heart ruined us evenly.

My sister feels comfort from this,
gets in the fetal position on my bed
and holds her chest like a toy.
My heart is healthy as a fist now.

The Anyjar alludes to the idea
that one sibling's deficiencies are created
by the other's harvests.
A sister is your apish parallel.

The next day my sister leaves
on a silver jet, bruised from conversation.
We are most tender in moments
of tremored goodbyes.

As she walks out the door,
I note that her head has expanded beautifully,
while my heart pulsates like a row
one petal at a time across the ocean.

Shi (Poetry)
for sms

Climate change will keep us here
                        b/n two milk-legs.
I invented you, wind
                        will show you how to tuck
your head in
how to keep safe from a volcano
the hurricanes of your mother
or another lyric moment.

Red water hot breath,
a specific outcome of surprise
blows your teeth.

I rock a baby gently through a moon cycle—the gauge is not for *hurt*
                        is not for *sensitivity*.
As if one end of the pole never had an opposite feeling.

This forgetting disease
doesn't take your intelligence away

(if you ever had it,
it was quietly sitting at the edge of the lake).

The disease is heady,
gets in there slices each layer of meatheadedness away

(if you ever had it,
one hand on the pole, one hand on the hook furiously biting your own cheeks).

No one here wants her future dictated.
Chimney out, smoke signals, flags.

When did "surrender" first appear as symbolism?
When did symbolism become sexy and terrifying and up in the air?

No one wants to hear what she can do about the problem.
I can't even think of the word "stop" without "demise" without a grammatical shift
or shifting focalization or meandering point-of-view.

For example, at the funeral
my sister named the coffin a "cock sling."

★★★

We sang,
I will build my own cock sling
I will have a simple cock sling
I will use a tree-nut cock sling

a locks from the inside cock sling
a bronze hole for breathing cock sling
a tough as water-loo cock sling

a howdy do you do it cock sling
a slip cover dip then lower cock sling
the two birds feed on the cock sling

the two birds shit and make love on the cock sling
the different compartments of the cock sling
this is where your head goes cock sling

this is where your pelvis goes cock sling
this is where your feet go cock sling

don't even think about the organs cock sling
don't even think about the bugs cock sling
don't even think about time travel cock sling

tear repellent shield on my cock sling
as soon as you hit the earth cock sling
everyone will be jealous of this cock sling, cock sling—

take care of our pain.

Do you feel the breeze between the branches?
The warm milk running up my thighs?

A paranoid woman gazes out the window of her limousine
while the sun beats like a humming bird on her tiny finger.

She says, they're coming to get her, that you try
to make everything simple but you can't.

Like I can't remember a word [
] that was once the metaphor.

The Last Elegics of the Year

I left the West coast heavy, unsatisfied
with the cold and crippling snow.

There, there
were strange movements

in every cabinet,
in every jar that I opened

I spent hours figuring
ways to soften the glass.

[*Dear Fay, I think of you in winter when I go to the hospital I think you are trying to tell me something about how I see the world how I imagine myself in spaces that I cannot access / this cave this cave of Fay not everything is what it is, but who could tell you? Who could power you up and over that small peninsula that we are all in danger of being accustomed to? / Sometimes I gloss over my fingers and remember that I've been trying to remember, get that damn vessel open for years ever since you left I make messes and neglect them for days for days I cry for reasons that are as real as they are imagined.*]

Photos of Fay, the dead woman of my dreams,
would fall onto my face,

leave me shivering at night, her hand
pulling at the hairs around my neck.

[*Dear Fay, This is where I say something about flying over states to catch you to find you lucid only to sit next to the self-proclaimed "King of Sausage" in Chicago on my flight I had the window and he had the aisle and the woman between us couldn't block my view as he touched himself as he rubbed and rubbed / I thought how horrible the world can be how obvious we are in our clichés and here I was flying out a couple hours / in a few minutes only a moment before it was "too late" before it was as silly as "she is already gone" like the yellow edge of a storm.*]

At hospice, I do not take a photograph
or watch others make-up the dead.
My aunt rubs lipstick on her cheeks,
tells her *mom, you look like a Queen.*

The next day, at her apartment,
I do not finger through her clothes
while we clean out her drawers,
look for the unknown parts of her life.

I tumble sweetly forward not as a child
running through Fay's summer roses,
not as a pelican who has opened her wings
underwater in an attempt to test fate.

I remember the conch shells
she stuffed in your pockets,
the algae sticking like ice.

The big idea shrivels then blooms.
I hear the graveyard bouquets
are lovely this time of year.

I am flooded with pictures.
Rosy-rubbed cheeks. Volcanic lips.
Your whole face erupts a quiet thought.

I wrote these lines on an airplane.
I wrote the title four days before you died.
This stanza was inserted, first, as a question

before I held your damp hands, moved
my fingers over your soft arms,
I pressed delete.

In the evening I walk out the door
like every possibility is a circle beyond me.

I sit in my childhood driveway, try to blend in
with the armadillos crawling under the house.

I hear the roots of a bougainvillea,
tear the pink shoots from their buds

and think of Fay's scissors, an instrument
stuck with rust and petal blood.

My father cried after
my mother's breasts were removed.

At his father's funeral, he threw the dirt
on the sweet pine before the coffin was lowered.

It's been a long time since we grieved with our limbs.
I hear under a cousin's breath, "when *he* died,

the rabbi asked if the family kept his amputated leg
from the war so that they could bury it with him."

I call you to tell you something else, good news,
but I've forgotten that we canceled your phone service.

[*Dear Fay, Bernard is dead. Rose is dead. I thought I would tell you how your birds sang,
then died the morning after you left them.*]

When I talk to Lover, I speak in concepts of the future,
as if the imminent tense will pull apart the shore.

Sometimes I think all this is a magic trick
that I must expose in order to understand art

(to blow this ship up to sell it as parts)
(to row and keep rowing until our arms fall off).

Lover, my origins reject the futurity of a sentence,
but those organs want to see a change, too.

Our studio without walls. Our open spaces.
I count your footsteps from the elevator

to the front door to the edge of the window
overlooking the new rocks of a new city.

These sentences are the forecast.
In the night I pray for the letters.

Tomorrow they will fall from the sky
and we will be swimming in the lees.

Notes

The line "the most uncreative act" from the poem "Anyjar on Repeat" was inspired by T.S. Eliot's essay "Tradition and the Individual Talent."

The lines *"if you feel what is inside that thing / you do not call it by the name by which it is known. / Everybody knows that by the way they do when they are in love."* from the poem, "On Geneology," is from Gertrude Stein's essay "Poetry & Grammar."

The title "Endings are not a Luxury" comes from Audre Lorde's essay "Poetry is Not a Luxury."

Acknowledgements

Thank you to the editors of the following journals who published earlier versions of these poems in the following: *Capitalism Nature Socialism (Volume 23, Issue 1)*, *Hawaii Review*, *Inknode, LOCUSPOINT, Spork Press* and *Tinfish Press*.

Thank you to the editors of the presses where several of these poems first appeared as chapbooks: *One Petal Row (Tinfish Press,* 2011) *and The Anyjar (Highway 101 Press,* 2011).

The poem "Messaging" won 1st place in the 2012 Ian MacMillan Award for Poetry and was published in *Hawaii Review*.

Thank you to Evan Nagle for being always my first and best reader, my honest companion and loving support system. You are my heart and without you, there are no poems.

Jonie, you are the reason.

Thank you to Susan M. Schultz for nurturing and believing, for your unwavering mentorship and friendship. Thank you to Shantel Grace, Jonathan Friedman and Christine Walsh for reading the very first versions of these poems. Thank you to Rajiv Mohabir for guidance and encouragement. Our conversations mean so much. Thank you to Dena Rash Guzman, Lee Ann Roripaugh, Prageeta Sharma, Brenda Shaughnessy and Cathy Wagner for their generosity. Thank you to Fay Ku for her beautiful and inspiring work that appears on the cover of this book, which I first encountered during her residency at The Honolulu Musuem of Art's Spalding House. And many thanks to Takiora Ingram and the Pacific Writers' Connection for sending me to the Hanalei Writers' Retreat in 2011, where the first Anyjar poem was conceived.